Dear Parent:
Your child's love of reading starts here!

Every child learns to read in a different way and at his or her own speed. Some go back and forth between reading levels and read favorite books again and again. Others read through each level in order. You can help your young reader improve and become more confident by encouraging his or her own interests and abilities. From books your child reads with you to the first books he or she reads alone, there are I Can Read Books for every stage of reading:

SHARED READING
Basic language, word repetition, and whimsical illustrations, ideal for sharing with your emergent reader

BEGINNING READING
Short sentences, familiar words, and simple concepts for children eager to read on their own

READING WITH HELP
Engaging stories, longer sentences, and language play for developing readers

READING ALONE
Complex plots, challenging vocabulary, and high-interest topics for the independent reader

ADVANCED READING
Short paragraphs, chapters, and exciting themes for the perfect bridge to chapter books

I Can Read Books have introduced children to the joy of reading since 1957. Featuring award-winning authors and illustrators and a fabulous cast of beloved characters, I Can Read Books set the standard for beginning readers.

A lifetime of discovery begins with the magical words "I Can Read!"

Visit www.icanread.com for information
on enriching your child's reading experience.

For Stan & Gilda ("Jill").
Keep on moving!
—H. P.

For Chloe, Scott, Ellie, Ben, and their new house.
They have been On the Move!—L. A.

Gouache and black pencil were used to prepare the full-color art.

I Can Read Book® is a trademark of HarperCollins Publishers.

Amelia Bedelia is a registered trademark of Peppermint Partners, LLC.

www.icanread.com

Library of Congress Control Number: 2017942449

ISBN 978-0-06-265886-9 (hardback)—ISBN 978-0-06-265885-2 (pbk ed.)

19 20 SCP 10 9 8

Greenwillow Books

Amelia Bedelia
• On the Move •

by Herman Parish ❀ pictures by Lynne Avril

Greenwillow Books, *An Imprint of* HarperCollins*Publishers*

Amelia Bedelia loved

to ride around town

with her parents.

It was fun to wonder

what was inside

other people's houses.

5

"Where are we going today?"
asked Amelia Bedelia.

"We are house hunting,"
said Amelia Bedelia's father.

Amelia Bedelia looked out her window.

"The houses are not hiding," she said.

"I see one, two, three, four.

Hunting for houses is easy."

"We are looking for houses
that are for sale,"
said Amelia Bedelia's mother.
"Look at that pretty Tudor house!"

FOR
SALE

"Our house has two doors,"
said Amelia Bedelia.

"We have a front door,
a back door,
and a garage door,"
said her father.

"That's right,"
said Amelia Bedelia.
"We live in
a three-door house."

9

"A Tudor-style house looks like an English home in the Middle Ages," explained Amelia Bedelia's mother. "There were many kings and queens in the Tudor family," said her father.

"Let's look for a colonial house,"
said Amelia Bedelia's father.
"Colonial-style homes have been popular
since the American Revolution,"
said Amelia Bedelia's mother.

"Hey, look!" said Amelia Bedelia's mother.

"That ranch is having an open house."

"Let's go in," said her father.

"Hooray!" said Amelia Bedelia.

"I love horses."

During the holidays,
Amelia Bedelia's parents
always had an open-house party.
Friends and neighbors
were free to stop by anytime.

It didn't look as though
there was a party here.
The house was quiet.
"Are we the first ones?"
said Amelia Bedelia.

The front door swung wide open.
"Welcome home!" said a smiling woman
with a name tag marked "Jill."

"Oh, I don't live here,"

said Amelia Bedelia.

"I live at my house.

We came to look at your house."

"Well, come right in," said Jill.

Jill gave Amelia Bedelia

a piece of paper.

"Here are some facts

about the house," she said.

"But I'm not the owner. I'm an agent."

Homes by Jill

Hi, I'm Jill, your real estate agent.
Let me find the perfect home
for you!!!

Style: Ranch
Built: 1952
Square Feet: 2,500

Bedrooms: 3
Bathrooms: 1.5
Hardwood floors and full,
finished basement
Acres: 1

Amelia Bedelia whispered

in her mother's ear.

Her mother smiled and said,

"No, sweetie, Jill is not a spy.

Not all agents are secret agents."

"Let me show you around," said Jill.

"What are you looking for?"

"We are running out of room,"
said Amelia Bedelia's mother.

"We need about six hundred more
square feet," said her father.

Amelia Bedelia knew

her father had two flat feet.

Why did he want

so many square ones?

8ft × 10ft = 80 sq ft

8'

10'

BEDROOM

2 × 300 sq' = 600 sq'

"Let's go upstairs," said Amelia Bedelia.

"I want to pick out my bedroom."

"A ranch-style house does not have

an upstairs," said her father.

"A ranch house is built like

a house on a ranch

out west."

"So where do we sleep?"

asked Amelia Bedelia.

"On this floor," said her mother.

"The house has hardwood floors,"

said Jill.

"It sure does!" said Amelia Bedelia.

"The floors are really hard."

Amelia Bedelia had an idea.

While her parents toured the house,

she would hunt for the horses.

"Where is the backyard?"

asked Amelia Bedelia.

"Go through the mudroom,"

said Jill, pointing to a door.

There wasn't any mud
in the mudroom—
just places to store coats and boots.

Amelia Bedelia opened the back door.

She could see the Tudor and the colonial.

She could see two dogs and a garden.

Where were the horses hiding?

"Come take a look downstairs," said Jill.

"This house has a full basement."

"Our basement was full once,"

said Amelia Bedelia.

"It flooded when a pipe broke."

"This basement is finished," said Jill.

"So was ours," said Amelia Bedelia.

"There is a huge rec room," said Jill.

"Our whole basement was wrecked," said Amelia Bedelia.

Amelia Bedelia's parents came downstairs.

"Aha! Here you are,"

said Amelia Bedelia's father.

"What a great recreation room,"

said Amelia Bedelia's mother.

"Lots of space for fun and games!"

said Amelia Bedelia.

"Thanks for stopping by," said Jill.

"Now that I know what you want,

I'll keep my ear to the ground."

Amelia Bedelia's stomach growled.

Jill must have heard it. Her father did.

"Lunchtime!" said Amelia Bedelia's father.

"I'm so hungry I could eat a horse."

"Then let's go," said Amelia Bedelia.

"You won't find a horse at this ranch."